Tasty Cooking For Two

This edition first published in 1973 by
Octopus Books Limited
59 Grosvenor Street, London W1

ISBN 0 7064 0209 X
© 1972 Octopus Books Pty Ltd
Distributed in USA by Crescent Books
a division of Crown Publishers Inc.
419 Park Avenue South, New York, NY 10016
Produced by Mandarin Publishers Limited
14 Westlands Road, Quarry Bay, Hong Kong
and printed in Hong Kong

Tasty Cooking For Two

SueRussell

Octopus Books

Contents

Metric Conversion Chart

Liquid Measurements

	Teaspoon	Tablespoon	Fluid Ounces	Cups	Liter
1 teaspoon	1 tsp.	1/3 T.	1/6 fl. oz.	1/64 C.	.05 deciliter
1 tablespoon	3 tsp.	1 T.	1/2 fl. oz.	1/16 C.	.15 deciliter
1 fluid ounce	6 tsp.	2 T.	1 fl. oz.	1/8 C.	.30 deciliter
1 cup	48 tsp.	16 T.	8 fl. oz.	1 C.	2 1/3 deciliter
1 pint		32 T.	16 fl. oz.	2 C.	4 3/4 deciliter
2 pints or 1 quart			32 fl. oz.	4 C.	9 1/2 deciliter
1/5 gallon			25 fl. oz.		
1 gallon or 4 quarts			128 fl. oz.	16 C.	3 4/5 liters
1 deciliter		8 T.	3½ fl. oz.	scant ½ C.	1/10 liter
1 demiliter			16 ¾ fl. oz.	2 1/8 C.	1/2 liter
1 liter or 1 quart, 2 fl. oz.			33 ½ fl. oz.	4 1/4 C.	10 deciliter

Dry Solid Measurements

1 gram	.035 ounces	
100 grams	3 1/2 ounces	almost 1/4 pound
1 ounce	28.35 grams	
1 teaspoon	5 grams	
2 tablespoons	30 grams	
1/2 pound	8 ounces	225 grams
1 pound	16 ounces	450 grams
250 grams	8 3/4 ounces	half pound +
1000 grams	34 1/2 ounces	1 kilogram
1 kilogram	2 1/4 pounds	
1 avoirdupois ounce	28 1/3 grams	

Weights and Measures

Measurements are given in cups, tablespoons and teaspoons as well as in pounds and ounces. The US Gill or Standard measuring cup has been used

1 cup	=	8 fluid ounces	=	16 tablespoons
1 tablespoon	=	15 milliliters		
1 teaspoon	=	5 milliliters		
1 pint	=	16 fluid ounces	=	2 cups

All measurements given are level.
To level a cup measure of solid ingredients, shake the cup gently and check the measurements at eye level. For an accurate spoon measure, level the ingredients off with the back of a palette, French or kitchen knife or with the back of a spatula.

Oven Temperature Guide

Description of Oven	Automatic Electric °F	Gas °F	Gas Regulo
Cool	200	200	0-½
Very Slow	250	250	½-1
Slow	300-325	300	1-2
Moderately Slow	325-350	325	2-3
Moderate	350-375	350	4
Moderately Hot	375-400	375	5
Hot	400-450	400	6-7
Very Hot	450-500	450	8-9

Eggs en Cocotte

Introduction

Cooking for Two is a very personal and perhaps revolutionary cookbook. It sets out clearly and simply the easiest, most economical way in which to prepare and cook delicious and exciting food for those with little time for cooking, but who wish to ensure that there is always superb food served at their table for two! Many cookbooks provide painstaking methods of preparing food for those with lots of leisure hours, but just how many cookbooks are aimed at a busy career woman or housewife? Instead of dishing up dreary, precooked food you have rushed round to buy at your local supermarket or delicatessen just as it is closing, by reading this book and devoting a little thought and preplanning to purchasing the right ingredients, you can serve delicious meals seven days a week with little extra effort. Try to plan your shopping so that you buy once a week in bulk, this cuts down on your valuable time, leaving you free to try out some of the chef-standard gourmet recipes in this book. Perhaps, once a week, choose a complete menu from your Cooking for Two, set the table with your best cutlery and linen, decorate it up with flowers and candles, put on your prettiest dress, and wait for your man's surprise and delight when you serve up a fabulous meal. It will pay off dividends! There is an exciting range of completely new Breakfast recipes you've never even dreamed of for intimate breakfasts. Or try out a breakfast party on your friends (just up the quantities per couple) served with Morning Glory — champagne and orange juice. Buy the cheapest champagne at your liquor store and add fresh-squeezed orange juice in equal quantities.

The Hors d'Oeuvres or Starters and Soups provide an exciting introduction to the Main Courses. These recipes, carefully planned for nourishment and eye appeal, some completely new, others traditional favorites, are all chosen for ease of preparation and their superb flavor. Delicate or filling Desserts round off the meal.

Many of the recipes contained in this book are ideal for cooking ahead, the day or night before. They can be stored in your refrigerator until ready for garnishing, heating and serving. The Salads and Vegetable recipes provide an ideal accompaniment to the meat, poultry and fish recipes of the Main Courses; some of them are meals in themselves. Try out some of the unique Salad recipes at your next barbecue or picnic.

Essentially this is a book for two people with quantities carefully chosen to avoid wastage, and to ensure that you, in your busy life, and with the minimum of fuss are a superb cook.

Breakfasts

Eggs en Cocotte

butter for greasing
salt
pepper
2 or 4 eggs
¼ oz butter (melted) per egg
¼ oz cream per egg

Grease individual ovenproof dishes (1 egg to a very small dish, or use a larger dish which will accommodate 2 eggs, if required) or one good-sized dish to contain 4 eggs. Grease dishes liberally with butter and sprinkle in salt and pepper. Break eggs into dishes. Pour melted butter and cream over the top. Set in a baking dish of hot water and bake in a moderate oven (375°F) for 8-10 minutes.
Eggs continue cooking after the dishes are removed from the oven, so do not overcook.
Variation: Before putting eggs into greased dish, put in a spoonful of chopped ham or lightly sautéed mushrooms.

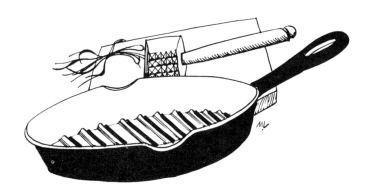

Soufflé Omelet

4 eggs, separated
1 tablespoon sugar
2 tablespoons cream
1½ tablespoons butter
1 cup sliced strawberries
1¼ tablespoons strawberry jam
confectioners' sugar

Beat egg yolks with sugar and cream.
Whisk whites until firm and fold into yolk mixture.
Heat omelet pan, add butter and when butter is sizzling
pour in egg mixture. Cook over low to moderate heat until
just set (1 to 1½ minutes), then brown under pre-heated
broiler
Spread with jam and sliced strawberries before folding.
Slide from pan, dust with sugar and serve.
NOTE: This omelet is best served as a late breakfast or
brunch, for it is really a dessert omelet.

French Omelet

4 eggs
1 tablespoon cold water
½ teaspoon salt
freshly ground black pepper
3 tablespoons butter

Break eggs into a bowl and whip thoroughly with a fork.
Add water and salt and pepper and mix.
Heat omelet pan over medium heat and add butter broken
into two or three pieces. When butter is sizzling, pour in egg
mixture. After about 15 seconds gently stir twice round the
pan with the back of a fork. Let set again for a few seconds,
then lift omelet from one side about 1/3 of the way across,
then fold in from the other side. Slip onto a warm plate and
serve at once.
NOTE: An omelet pan should be heavy, and have rounded
edges. An 8-inch diameter pan will hold 4 eggs, sufficient for
2 for breakfast. If possible the pan should be kept for omelets
and pancakes only and not washed with soap, but merely
wiped out with some paper or a clean cloth.

Variation: Tomato Omelet: Cut 2 medium tomatoes into
¼-inch slices. Sauté lightly in ½ tablespoon butter, and
sprinkle with salt and pepper. Place across centre of omelet
as it is just cooked, then fold as for basic omelet. Serve
sprinkled with finely chopped parsley

Continental Breakfast

orange or grapefruit juice, freshly squeezed
bread rolls, preferably the knotted ones sprinkled with poppy
   or sesame seeds
butter
jam
2 mild cheeses
ham, thinly sliced
2 apples and 2 oranges
strong, black, freshly brewed coffee
1 cup milk

Brew coffee using 4 tablespoons medium grind coffee and
2 cups water. Dampen rolls with water, or use frozen rolls.
Place in moderate oven (350°F) for 5-7 minutes.
Serve juice.
Heat milk until almost boiling, bring to the table with coffee
in a separate jug. Serve hot rolls with butter, jam, cheeses
(such as Bel Paese, Edam, Gouda) and ham slices, rolled up
and secured with a wooden pick.
Fresh oranges and apples can be served; whether eaten or
not, they look fresh and bright on the breakfast table. Pour
half milk, half coffee into big breakfast mugs, or, if preferred,
serve black coffee made according to taste. You may like to
add a boiled or poached egg to this breakfast.

Eggs and Candied Ham

1 tablespoon butter
2½ tablespoons pineapple juice
2 slices ham, ¼-inch thick
1¼ tablespoons brown sugar
1 or 2 eggs per person

Melt butter in an ovenproof dish. Add pineapple juice. Put ham slices in dish and sprinkle with brown sugar. Cook in a moderately hot oven (375°F) for 10 minutes. When ham is almost ready, heat a skillet containing ¼-inch cooking oil until it sizzles when a drop of water is flicked into it.
Break eggs gently into oil, keeping them apart if possible. Baste them while they cook with hot oil until white over yolk is set. Lift eggs from oil with an egg turner and drain well. Serve with ham.
Alternative: Serve eggs with bacon: Fry bacon in greased pan over moderate heat, turning once, and cooking until well-browned but still moist. Keep warm while cooking eggs.

Eggs in the Shell

1 or 2 eggs per person

Bring a small saucepan of water to the boil; add a teaspoon of
salt and 1¼ tablespoons of vinegar as this will stop the white
escaping if eggs crack. Do not use eggs straight from the
refrigerator as these will burst if plunged straight into boiling
water.
Take room temperature eggs and gently lower on a spoon into
the boiling water.
Allow eggs to simmer gently for 4-5 minutes.
Remove from pan and serve immediately with salt and pepper
and hot buttered toast fingers.

Scrambled Eggs

2 tablespoons butter
4 eggs
salt and pepper
a little chopped parsley

Melt a large piece of butter in a saucepan (preferably a
non-stick pan) and add the eggs which have been very well
beaten and seasoned.
Cook over a low heat, until eggs start to thicken, add some
more butter and keep on stirring for another 30 seconds
then remove from heat.
Serve at once on hot buttered toast, sprinkled with parsley.

From the Broiler

Broiled bacon, kidneys, baby lamb loin chops, sausages and tomato, in various combinations, make a sustaining and appetizing breakfast.

Suitable portions for each person would be two small lean chops and half a tomato, or two half kidneys with 2 slices of bacon with tomato. You will decide quantity and variety according to appetite.

To broil, pre-heat broiler at highest heat for five minutes so that meats are sealed quickly and juices retained. Chops should be trimmed of excess fat, sealed on each side.

Sausages should be well-pricked, and, depending on size, may need to be cooked for as long as 15 minutes.

Tomatoes should be cut in half, crosswise, and placed under a hot broiler for about 5 minutes. Bacon also requires a few minutes under a hot broiler, and should be turned just once. You may prefer to cook bacon, sausages and tomatoes in a skillet.

First Courses

Stuffed Peaches

3 oz cream cheese
1¼ tablespoons light raisins (plump in boiling water
    beforehand)
1¼ tablespoons crushed walnuts
1 large unblemished ripe peach or 2 halves of canned peaches
2 crisp lettuce leaves

Mix the cheese, raisins and nuts and make into about 6 small
balls. If these balls are very soft, chill the mixture for a short
time.
Arrange the peaches on a lettuce leaf in individual bowls
or glasses and place 3 cheese balls into each.

Sautéed Shrimp

butter
8 fresh large shrimp, unshelled
salt and freshly ground black pepper
fresh parsley and fennel
lemon juice

Melt enough butter in a small heavy pan to cover the
bottom of the pan well. When the butter is bubbling, add
the shrimp in their shells. Cook gently for about 5 minutes
on each side until they are pink.
Remove pan from heat, shell the shrimp — but leave on the
tails. Season to taste with salt and pepper, a little parsley
and fennel and lemon juice.
Serve with crusty French bread.

Cold Consommé

Chill a 16 ounce can of good quality beef consommé and
serve in individual dishes topped with a dollop of sour cream
garnished with chopped chives.

Moules Marinière

3 lbs fresh mussels
¾ cup dry white wine or cider
1 small onion, chopped
1 clove garlic, chopped
½ celery stalk, sliced
a handful of chopped parsley

Make sure your mussels come from a reliable source, i.e.
from unpolluted water, as mussels (like oysters) tend to
collect any impurities present in the water.
Discard any mussels that have holes in them or are open.
Remove the beards with a knife and scrape off any marine
growths like barnacles or small shells which may be adhering
to the shells. Scrub them well and wash in plenty of cold
water until the water is clean and free of grit.
Place them in a wide pan with the wine, and vegetables and
cook over high heat until the shells open. Remove from the
heat the minute the shells open.
Serve immediately in a warmed tureen with the cooking
liquid poured over them. It is a good idea to provide another
plate for the empty shells.

Gazpacho/Chicken Liver Pâté

Cream Cheese Celery Sticks

large celery sticks cut into 3-inch lengths
4 oz cream cheese
1¼ tablespoons finely chopped gherkin or dill pickle
2 slices ham, finely chopped
salt and pepper

Wash celery. Beat cheese until smooth then stir in the gherkins
and ham. Blend well. Season to taste.
Fill the celery sticks with the mixture. Serve cold.

Eggplant Dip

1 medium eggplant
1 clove garlic, chopped and crushed
salt
freshly ground black pepper
olive oil
1 teaspoon lemon juice
1¼ tablespoons finely chopped parsley

This can be served as an appetizer, entrée or as part of a salad.
Broil the eggplant until it is soft throughout. Scoop out the
flesh and mash it in a dish with a wooden spoon, mixing in
the garlic, salt and pepper. Add very slowly some olive oil
until you have a thickish purée, then stir in the lemon juice
and some parsley.
Serve with slices of rye bread.

Oeufs en Gelée

2 eggs
1 thick slice ham
10 oz can beef consomme with gelatin or madrilene
2 teaspoons sherry
a little tarragon

Carefully poach the eggs in boiling salted water to which you
have added a dash of vinegar or lemon juice. Take them out
before the yolks are set, they should be rather runny. To
stop them cooking beyond the desired point, add cold water
to the pan in which they are cooking, then remove them.
Put half the ham into each of two cocottes and carefully
place an egg in each, being very careful not to break the yolk.
Cover with enough consommé, to which you have added the
sherry, to just cover the eggs. Sprinkle with a little chopped
tarragon and chill. Serve in the cocottes.

Mushrooms Vinaigrette

4 oz. fresh mushrooms
3¾ tablespoons olive oil
1 tablespoon lemon juice
1 clove garlic, finely chopped and crushed
salt and freshly ground black pepper
1 teaspoon finely chopped parsley

Wipe mushrooms and slice — do not remove the stalks.
Combine oil, lemon juice, garlic, salt and pepper and parsley.
Pour the dressing over the mushrooms and make sure they are
coated on all sides.
Chill for several hours before serving. The raw mushrooms
are extremely absorbent, you may have to put some more
of the dressing on them.

Egg and Cheese Soup

1 pint chicken stock
1 egg yolk
1¼ tablespoons finely grated cheese

Heat the stock to boiling point. Beat the egg yolk well with
the cheese. Pour about half the stock into the mixture
slowly, return this to the pan with the rest of the stock and
bring almost to the boil, stirring continuously.
Serve hot.

Mushrooms Vinaigrette

Escargots Bourguignonne

2 dozen canned snails
½ cup very finely chopped parsley
1 shallot, very finely chopped
1 clove garlic, chopped and pounded
½ cup unsalted butter (1 stick)
freshly ground black pepper
salt

You will need specially designed dishes to cook your snails
in the oven. These are circular and have an indentation to hold
each snail, alternatively you can use the little snail pots
called 'godets', which are very much like an egg cup and hold
one snail each, they dispense with the necessity for special
eating utensils and are also less likely to tip over on the way
from the oven to the table.
Drain snails well. Mix together the parsley, shallot and garlic.
Work this into the butter and season with pepper and the
smallest pinch of salt (canned snails are usually quite salty).
Put a little knob of butter into each shell (or godet), add the
snail, press it in quite firmly and then add more butter so
that the shell is as full as possible.
Put the filled shells open end up in special snail pans, cover
with aluminium foil and cook in a moderately hot oven
(375°F) for about 8 minutes. Be very careful not to let the
snails tip over for if they do all the garlic butter will spill
out.
Serve hot with hot garlic bread

Garbanzo (Chick Pea) Soup

½ cup chick peas, soaked overnight
olive oil
1 clove garlic, chopped and crushed
½ onion, peeled and sliced
½ green pepper, seeded, cored and chopped
1 anchovy fillet, chopped
2 tomatoes, peeled and chopped
pinch rosemary
salt and pepper
½ cup small noodles

Put the soaked chick peas in a pan with 2 pints of cold water
and bring to the boil. Simmer gently until peas are tender but
not mushy. Strain and retain cooking liquor.
Saute the onion, garlic, anchovy and green pepper in olive oil
in a frying pan (skillet) until tender but not browned.
Add the tomatoes and rosemary and simmer gently for about
10 minutes. Add this to the chick peas and ½ pint of the
liquid they have been cooking in. Add seasoning to taste and
bring to the boil. Put in the noodles and continue simmering
until tender. Serve hot.

Shrimp in Cream Sauce

¾ lb shrimp, cooked and shelled
freshly ground black pepper
pinch nutmeg
3 tablespoons butter
¾ cup thick cream
¼ cup brandy
1 teaspoon finely chopped parsley
lemon wedges

Season the shrimp with pepper and nutmeg.
Heat the butter in a small pan (skillet) and saute shrimp
over gentle heat for 3 minutes. Flame the shrimp with the
brandy (warm gently in a large spoon or ladle, ignite and
pour flaming brandy into the pan). When the flames have
gone out, reduce heat to low and cook for a further 2 minutes.
Increase the heat and add the cream. Cook until the cream
thickens, shake the pan and stir the sauce. Stir in the parsley.
Serve hot on plain boiled rice, garnished with lemon wedges.

Stuffed Avocado Pears

1 avocado pear
1 teaspoon white wine vinegar
1 very finely chopped anchovy
½ teaspoon paprika
2½ tablespoons cream
salt and pepper
lemon wedges

Remove the stone from the avocado. Scoop out the meat and
mash well with a wooden spoon.
Add the vinegar, anchovy, paprika and cream to the mashed
flesh and mix well. Season to taste.
Pile into the empty shells and serve chilled, garnished with
lemon wedges.

Avgolemono (Egg and Lemon Soup)

1¼ pints chicken broth
salt and pepper
1¼ tablespoons uncooked rice
1 egg
juice of 1 lemon, strained
parsley

Boil the broth, season to taste with salt and pepper. Add rice to the boiling broth and simmer till tender, covered, about 12 minutes.
As the soup cooks, beat the egg then gradually beat in the lemon juice and then add to this mixture very slowly ¾ cup of the boiling broth. Add this to the soup while it is still cooking, stirring all the time. Cook gently for 3 minutes and remove from heat. Allow to stand for 2 minutes before serving garnished with chopped parsley.

French Onion Soup

2 tablespoons butter
1 large onion, thinly sliced
2 teaspoons flour
2 cups beef broth or bouillon
1 teaspoon sugar
salt
freshly ground black pepper
French bread
grated cheese

Heat the butter in a heavy pan, add the onion and cook, stirring continuously until the onion is soft and golden, do not overcook. Stir in the flour then slowly stir in the broth or bouillon. Add the sugar. Season to taste. Cover and simmer gently for 20 minutes.

Toast some slices of French bread and sprinkle generously with grated cheese. Grill until cheese melts and bubbles. Top each bowl of soup with a slice of toast. Serve hot.

French Onion Soup

Iced Cucumber Soup

½ fresh cucumber
8 oz plain yogurt
1 cup iced water
1 tablespoon olive oil
1 teaspoon chopped mint
2½ tablespoons light raisins, plumped in hot water beforehand
2 cloves garlic, 1 chopped finely and 1 crushed
salt

Peel and dice cucumber and sprinkle with salt. In another
bowl, beat the yogurt until smooth and add the iced water.
Drain the cucumber and dry with a tea towel.
Rub another bowl with the piece of crushed garlic. Put the
oil in this bowl and stir in the yogurt, water, cucumber, mint,
light raisins and chopped garlic; chill before serving.

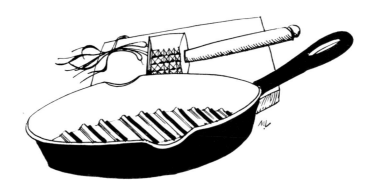

Vichyssoise

1 cup peeled and sliced leeks (white part only)
1 fairly large potato, peeled and sliced
½ onion, sliced
4 sprigs parsley, tied together
1 cup chicken stock (use a stock cube)
1 cup milk
salt
white pepper
chives for garnish

Put the vegetables in a saucepan with the parsley and add the
stock. Cook gently until all the vegetables are tender.
Discard the parsley and press the vegetables through a sieve.
This will be a little difficult, so moisten them with a little of
the milk. Gradually add more milk until the soup is the
consistency of thin cream, season to taste with salt and
pepper. Can be served either hot or chilled.
Serve garnished with chopped chives.

Zucchini à la Grècque

1 lb small zucchini
¾ cup olive oil
juice of 1 lemon
1 cup water
bay leaf
2 pinches thyme
a few crushed peppercorns
¼ teaspoon coriander seeds
2 medium tomatoes, skinned and chopped
1 clove garlic, crushed and minced
salt

Wash the zucchini and trim off any damaged skin. Remove
both ends and slice the zucchini into inch-long pieces. Place
in a colander and sprinkle with salt. Let stand for an hour to
drain, then rinse and dry.
Bring the oil, lemon juice, water, bay leaf, thyme, peppercorns
and a few coriander seeds to the boil, put in the tomatoes and
dried zucchini. Cook quite fast for 20 minutes uncovered.
Drain off any remaining liquid. Add the garlic, sprinkle with salt
and chill before serving.

Zucchini a la Grecque

Gazpacho

1 large ripe tomato
¼ cucumber
¼ green pepper
3 shallots or green onions
1¼ tablespoons olive oil
1 teaspoon white wine vinegar
½ cup chilled water
1 clove garlic, crushed
salt and pepper
ice cubes

A refreshing summer soup.

Skin tomato by plunging into boiling water then peeling.
Purée the tomato in a blender or press through a sieve. Peel
and finely dice the cucumber. Dice green pepper finely.
Thinly slice the shallots.
Stir the vegetables into the tomato purée along with the oil,
vinegar and chilled water. Add the garlic and season to taste,
chill well before serving. Serve with an ice cube in each bowl.

Chicken Liver Pâté

½ lb chicken livers
4 tablespoons butter
2 tablespoons sherry or brandy
1 clove garlic, chopped and crushed
pinch thyme
pinch mixed spice
salt
freshly ground black pepper
melted butter or chicken fat

Clean the livers well, removing any membrane or tubes.
Sauté gently in half the butter for 3 minutes, they should
still be pink inside. Remove the livers and add the sherry or
brandy to the pan.
Mash the livers well with a wooden spoon, add a little salt
and pepper, garlic, the rest of the butter and spice and herbs.
Stir in the liquid from the pan and spoon the paté into a
small earthenware bowl. Pour on a little melted butter or
chicken fat to cover the top to seal in the flavor. Chill well.
Serve with hot toast
This makes more than enough for two, but keeps well in
the refrigerator for a day or so.

Main Courses

Cold Mackerel in White Wine

1 small mackerel, ready-to-cook
¾ cup dry white wine or cider
¾ cup water
1 small onion, sliced
fennel
strip of lemon peel
4 whole peppercorns
bay leaf
salt
French mustard
chopped parsley

Simmer wine, water, onion, a little fennel, lemon peel, peppercorns, bay leaf and a pinch of salt together for 10 minutes, strain and let the liquid cool. Poach the cleaned mackerel in this bouillon as gently as possible for about 10 minutes or until the fish is no longer pink in the middle. Carefully lift the fish from the liquid and remove all skin. Divide the fish into two fillets and remove bones. Strain ¾ cup of the liquid and stir it into a little French mustard. Pour this over the fish and garnish with chopped parsley. Chill before serving.
Serve with cucumber salad.

Cold Marinated Tuna

1 lb tuna, cut in two slices
flour for coating
½ cup olive oil
1 small carrot, peeled and thinly sliced
1 small onion, thinly sliced
a little finely chopped parsley
salt
few whole peppercorns
a little mustard
1 bay leaf
1 cup white wine
½ cup white vinegar
juice ¼ lemon

Lightly coat the fish with flour and fry the fish in olive oil
on both sides until brown.
Put the fish aside in a small earthenware dish. Fry the carrot,
onion and parsley lightly in the oil in which you fried the fish.
Add a pinch of salt, a few peppercorns, mustard to taste,
bay leaf, wine, vinegar and lemon juice. Bring this to the boil
and simmer for 10 minutes. Pour over the fish and chill for
at least a day before serving.
Serve with salad.

Trout with Almonds

2 cleaned trout, each about 10-inches long
salt and freshly ground black pepper
flour
½ cup butter (1 stick)
1 teaspoon lemon juice
¼ cup toasted slivered almonds
parsley
lemon slices

Sprinkle the trout both inside and out with salt and pepper
and toss lightly in flour.
Heat half the butter in a heavy pan and cook the fish until
well browned on both sides. Put aside and keep warm.
Add the rest of the butter to the pan with the lemon juice
and toasted almonds, simmer for a few minutes and pour
over the fish. Garnish with parsley and lemon wedges and
serve hot.

Herring Salad

2 salted herrings
milk and water
olive oil
white wine vinegar
1 egg, hard-boiled and chopped
a few capers

Soak the herrings overnight in half milk and water to cover.
Drain and dress with vinegar and oil. Sprinkle with egg and
garnish with a few capers.
Serve chilled with salad.

Sole Véronique

2 fillets sole
½ small onion, sliced
bay leaf
4 peppercorns
2 teaspoons lemon juice
2 tablespoons butter
1¼ tablespoons flour
¾ cup milk
salt and pepper
handful of peeled white grapes.

Roll the fillets and secure with a wooden pick. Place in a
greased ovenproof dish with onion, bay leaf, peppercorns and
lemon juice. Add enough water to half-cover the fish. Cover
and cook in a moderate oven (350°F) until tender, about
25-30 minutes.
Put fish aside and keep hot, reserve ½ cup of the liquid. Melt
butter in a small saucepan, stir in flour and cook for 1 minute.
Remove from heat and slowly add the milk and the reserved
liquid which has been reduced by fast boiling to half its
original quantity. Return to heat, bring to the boil and simmer
until smooth and thick. Stir constantly. Season to taste.
To serve, pour sauce over fish and arrange grapes around it.

Plaki (Mediterranean Fish Stew)

1 medium size firm-fleshed fish (mullet is suitable) about ¾ lb
1 large onion, sliced
1 clove garlic, crushed
olive oil
1 lb can tomatoes
1 lemon
2 tablespoons white wine
3¾ tablespoons chopped parsley
extra sprigs of parsley for garnish

The fish should be cleaned and the head removed.
Cut the fish into 2-inch pieces. Saute the fish, onion and
garlic lightly in a little oil. Add the tomatoes with the juice, wine
and chopped parsley and ½ the lemon cut in slices. Cover and
simmer slowly until the fish is tender, about 15-20 minutes.
Remove any bones and the remains of the lemon slices.
Serve on a bed of hot white rice garnished with a little chopped
parsley and the remaining ½ lemon cut into wedges.

Goulash

1 lb stewing beef or veal
1 large onion, sliced
oil
1 tablespoon paprika
1 small can tomato paste
salt
yogurt or sour cream for serving.

Trim the meat carefully and cut into bite-sized pieces. Cook
meat and onion in a little oil until the meat is slightly
browned and the onions transparent.
Add paprika, tomato paste and enough cold water to cover.
Stir well, add salt to taste and simmer gently until the meat is
tender, about 1½ hours.
Serve with plain boiled potatoes, rice or noodles, topped with
a dollop of sour cream or yogurt.

Carpetbag Steak

1 lb rump or fillet steak, about 3-inches thick
salt and pepper
1 doz oysters
butter

Cut the steak into two pieces. Make a pocket in each piece with
a very sharp knife, season the pocket with salt and pepper and
stuff half the drained oysters into each pocket. Fasten the
pockets with small skewers.
Pan fry the steaks in butter. Serve immediately, dotted with
butter and accompanied with freshly cooked vegetables or
tossed green salad.

Pepper Steak

2 pieces steak (fillet, rump or sirloin)
1 tablespoon whole black peppercorns
4 tablespoons butter
1 tablespoon olive oil
2 teaspoons brandy
1 teaspoon butter

Crush the peppercorns coarsely with a rolling pin. Press these
into the steak on both sides and let stand for about an hour.
Put steaks in the heated butter and oil in a heavy pan and
cook quickly on both sides (this is to seal in the juices). Then
cook to your taste. Put aside and keep hot.
Stir the brandy into the pan juices and bring to the boil,
scraping the pan. Remove from heat and stir in the extra
butter. Pour this sauce over the steaks and serve
immediately with vegetables or tossed green salad.

Pepper Steak

Steak Diane

12 oz fillet steak, 1-inch thick
freshly ground black pepper
6 tablespoons butter
1¼ tablespoons Worcestershire sauce
1¼ tablespoons cream
1¼ tablespoons chopped parsley
a clove garlic, crushed

The steak should be bought 1-inch thick and then pounded
till very thin. Cut into two pieces.
Lightly season the steak on both sides with the pepper. Put
butter in a heavy pan and when sizzling add the steak. While
the steak is cooking on one side, rub garlic into the top of it
with a wooden spoon. Turn the steak and add the
Worcestershire sauce to the pan, moving the steak around in
the juices. When cooked to taste, transfer to a plate and
sprinkle with parsley. Add the cream to juices in pan, stir and heat
thoroughly and pour the sauce over the steak. Serve immediately
with tossed green salad.

Turkish Poached Eggs

1 pint plain yogurt
2 teaspoons white wine vinegar
1 clove garlic, finely chopped and crushed
salt
4 eggs
1¼ tablespoons butter
paprika

Beat the yogurt in a bowl till smooth and then stir in the
vinegar, garlic, and salt. Pour the mixture into individual
serving dishes and top each with 2 poached eggs.
Melt the butter in a small pan, add just enough paprika to
color it, season with salt to taste. Garnish the eggs and
yogurt with this mixture and serve immediately.
This may also be served cold.

Spaghetti Etcetera

4 oz spaghetti
plenty of boiling, salted water
4 tablespoons olive oil.
½ lb fresh mushrooms, wiped and sliced
2 medium onions, thinly sliced
2 cloves garlic, chopped and crushed
5 anchovy fillets, chopped
3 slices lean bacon, chopped
6 black olives
a handful of fresh parsley, roughly chopped
grated Parmesan cheese

Cook the spaghetti in the boiling, salted water until tender.
Meanwhile, heat some oil and cook the mushrooms, onions,
garlic, anchovy fillets, bacon, olives and parsley gently in it
for about 15 minutes in a covered frying pan.
Serve the spaghetti topped with this mixture and sprinkled
with grated Parmesan cheese.

Spaghetti Etcetera

Chili Con Carne

2½ tablespoons oil
1 medium onion, chopped
1 clove garlic, crushed
¾ lb best ground beef
6 oz can tomato paste
3 dried red chilis or 2 teaspoons chili powder
bay leaf
pinch thyme
salt and pepper
10 oz can kidney beans

Heat a little oil in a saucepan, add chopped onion and garlic
and cook till soft. Add the meat and cook until the meat
changes color, stirring frequently. Stir in the tomato paste,
dried chilis or chili powder and sufficient cold water
(about ¾ cup) to cover the meat. Add a bay leaf and a pinch
of thyme and season to taste.
Simmer gently, uncovered, stirring frequently and adding a
little water if the sauce reduces too much, for about an hour.
Add the drained kidney beans and simmer for a further 30
minutes. Keep the juice from the beans and use a little of
this if the chili con carne becomes dry.
This dish improves if cooked the day before and reheated.
Serve hot with boiled rice.

Spaghetti Bolognese

2 tablespoons olive oil
1 small onion, chopped
1 clove garlic, crushed
¾ lb best ground beef
2 medium mushrooms, wiped and sliced
½ glass red wine
6 oz can tomato paste
1 lump sugar
bay leaf
pinch basil
water or stock
4 oz spaghetti
plenty of boiling, salted water
grated Parmesan cheese

In a small, heavy pan heat some oil and sauté the onion and
garlic till soft. Add the meat and mushrooms and cook till
the meat changes color. Add the wine and allow this to
bubble till reduced by half, turning the meat all the time.
Add the tomato paste, sugar, bay leaf, basil and enough stock
or water to give a thinnish consistency as the sauce will
reduce considerably with cooking. The sauce should be
simmered very gently for as long as you like (at least ½ an
hour – but the longer the better). It can be left in a very
slow oven for a few hours. This sauce improves if cooked the
day before and reheated.
Serve very hot with spaghetti cooked in plenty of salted,
boiling water and then well drained. Top with grated Parmesan
cheese.

Wiener Schnitzel

Cooking time: 4-5 minutes

2 veal steaks
seasoned flour
1 egg, beaten
8-10 tablespoons dry breadcrumbs
1 stick (½ cup) butter
lemon wedges for garnish

Trim the veal into a neat shape and snip around the edge
with kitchen scissors, to prevent the schnitzel from curling
up during frying. Beat veal lightly with a meat cleaver or
wooden rolling pin until ⅛ - ¼ inch thin.
Place seasoned flour, beaten egg and dry breadcrumbs on
three individual plates.
Heat butter in a heavy frying pan.
Working quickly, dip the veal into the flour until coated
completely, then dip into the beaten egg, then into the
breadcrumbs. Press breadcrumbs on firmly with a knife and
put veal into the frying pan.
Fry quickly for 1-2 minutes until golden, turn over and fry
the other side 1-2 minutes. The perfect coating should
bubble in a few places.
Drain schnitzel well on absorbent kitchen paper and serve at
once garnished with lemon wedges and accompanied with
potato salad and green salad.

Wiener Schnitzel

58

Braised Garlic Lamb

2 lamb leg (lamb steak) chops
2½ tablespoons bacon fat.
salt
freshly ground black pepper
16 cloves of garlic
1 tablespoon flour
½ cup beef broth
1¼ tablespoons tomato purée

Fry the chops lightly on each side in the fat in a heavy frying
pan (skillet), season and place the garlic cloves (unpeeled)
around the chops. Cook for 3 minutes.
Sprinkle the flour over the chops, pour in the broth and the
tomato purée and simmer gently till the chops are tender.
Add some more stock if necessary. Serve the meat surrounded
by the whole garlic cloves.

Peasant Ragôut

1 lb lamb chops suitable for stewing – shoulder (arm) chops
   are good
2 lb large white onions, peeled and roughly chopped
2 cloves garlic, crushed
2½ tablespoons olive oil
1 pint red wine
6 oz can tomato paste
salt and freshly ground black pepper
bay leaf

Trim the meat of all fat, leave any bones in the meat as these
can easily be removed later on. Cut the meat into bite sized
pieces.
Sauté the meat, onions and garlic in oil until the onions are
soft and the meat lightly browned all over.
Add the remaining ingredients and simmer as slowly as
possible until the ragôut has the consistency of jam, about
3-4 hours.

This may also be cooked in a casserole in a very slow oven.
Remove the bones before serving.
Serve with boiled new potatoes or rice.

Simple Cassoulet

¾ lb lamb chops suitable for stewing
1 onion, sliced
1¼ tablespoons bacon fat
6 oz can tomato paste
¾ cup dried white beans, soaked overnight.
1½ cups broth or water (you may substitute ¼ cup of this
    with ¼ cup of red wine)
1 carrot, scraped and sliced
1 parsnip, scraped and sliced
1 stalk celery, sliced
sprig of parsley
bay leaf
pinch thyme
freshly ground black pepper
salt

Sauté meat, which has been trimmed and cut into bite-sized
pieces, and onion in the fat until meat is lightly browned and
onion is transparent.
Pour in a little water or stock, stir in the tomato paste. Add
the rest of the water or stock, the drained beans, carrot,
parsnip, celery, parsley, bay leaf, thyme and a grind of black
pepper.
Bring gently to the boil and simmer covered gently until
meat is very tender — about 2 hours. Add salt to taste and
simmer gently for a further 30 minutes uncovered.
Serve hot.

Simple Cassoulet

Bocconcini

4 small very thin escalopes of veal (veal round steak)
salt and pepper
2 pieces raw ham the same size as the escalopes
2 slices Gruyere cheese
1 egg
breadcrumbs
6 tablespoons butter
4 slices fried bread

Beat veal until 1/8 inch thick, trim into neat shapes and
season with salt and pepper.
On each piece of seasoned veal, place half a piece of raw ham
and half a slice of Gruyere cheese. Roll and tie with string.
Roll each piece in beaten egg and breadcrumbs and sauté
in butter till golden. They are ready when the cheese is just
melting.
Remove the string and serve each piece on a hot slice of fried
bread.

Veal with Apples and Cream

2 Granny Smith apples
2 veal steaks
salt and pepper
butter
1 shallot or green onion, finely chopped
2 teaspoons brandy or Calvados
3¾ tablespoons cream

Peel and core the apples and cut into small cubes. Cook
them gently with a little water in a covered pan.
Season the veal. Heat a small piece of butter in a frying pan
and just as it begins to turn brown, put in the veal and saute quickly
for 2 minutes on each side. Reduce heat and then saute for
3 minutes on each side.
Put aside and keep hot. Fry the shallot in the pan, add the
brandy and flame it. Mash the cooked apples and add to the
pan. Stir in the cream to make a smooth sauce. Season if
necessary.
Pour the sauce over the veal and serve at once.

Turkish Lamb Shanks

2 lamb shanks (have the butcher chop through the bone
    for you)
flour
5 tablespoons oil
salt and pepper
1 medium onion, chopped
1 clove garlic, crushed
1 green pepper, chopped
1 teaspoon cumin seeds
1 teaspoon whole black peppercorns
15 oz can tomato juice
juice ½ lemon

Roll the shanks lightly in a little flour and brown lightly in
the oil. Add the onion and cook until soft.
Add the remaining ingredients and simmer as slowly as
possible until the meat is falling off the bone (at least
3 hours).
Garnish with lemon wedges.

Turkish Lamb Shanks

Shish Kebabs

¾ lb lean lamb leg chops (lamb leg steaks), cut in 1½-inch
    cubes
½ cup plain yogurt
freshly ground black pepper
pinch each thyme, rosemary and oregano
6 mushroom caps
2½ tablespoons olive oil
¼ teaspoon salt
2 green peppers, cut into 1½-inch squares
1 slice bacon, cut into 1½-inch squares
6 small tomatoes, whole
bay leaves
6 small onions, whole
lemon juice

Marinate the meat in a mixture of yogurt, pepper, thyme,
rosemary and oregano for at least 2 hours, turning at least
once. Also marinate the mushroom caps in oil seasoned with
salt. Make sure that both sides of the mushroom caps are
coated with the dressing.
Remove the meat from the marinade and drain. Place pieces
of meat on skewers, alternating meat, green peppers, bacon,
mushroom caps, tomatoes, bay leaves and onions. Sprinkle
lightly with lemon juice and broil over charcoal or under
a hot broiler.
Serve on a bed of parsley or shredded lettuce with wedges
of lemon.

Moussaka

2 eggs, beaten
1 cup milk
salt
freshly ground black pepper
1 large very ripe tomato, peeled and chopped
1 teaspoon sugar
1 clove garlic, chopped and crushed
1¼ tablespoons chopped onion
pinch of basil
2 onions, sliced
3 small eggplant sliced but not peeled
oil
2 cups left-over roast leg of lamb (or roast beef) finely
    ground
½ cup broth

This dish is delicious hot or cold and is an ideal way to use
left-over lamb or beef.

Add the beaten eggs to the milk, season with salt and pepper
and cook gently until a thick custard forms. Put aside to cool.
Make a tomato sauce by cooking together the tomato, sugar,
garlic, chopped onion and basil over gentle heat until most
of the water has cooked out and you are left with a very
thick sauce. Mash with a wooden spoon and season to taste.
Fry the sliced onions and eggplant in oil till the onion is
golden and the eggplant tender.
Cover the bottom of a small rectangular cake or loaf tin
with a film of oil and wipe the sides of the tin with oil
also. Make alternate layers of eggplant, mixture and ground
meat until you have used all these ingredients. Pour in the
broth, spread the tomato sauce over the top and then the
egg mixture. Cook in a moderate oven (350°F) for 1 hour.

Garlic Chicken

3 tablespoons butter
1¼ tablespoons olive oil
half a chicken jointed or several joints
½ lemon
salt and pepper
20 plump, fresh garlic cloves – peeled but not crushed

Melt oil and butter in a heavy frying pan. Rub the chicken
with the lemon and season with salt and pepper. Cook the
garlic and the chicken over a moderate heat to seal in the
juices but see that the chicken doesn't brown too fast. Turn
from time to time, the chicken should be ready in about 25
minutes.
Serve hot with the golden brown garlic pieces and a crisp lettuce
salad.

Lemon Garlic Kidneys

6 lamb kidneys
salt and pepper
1 clove garlic, chopped
1 tablespoon olive oil
juice of ½ a lemon

Skin and core the kidneys and cut into ½-inch slices. Season
with salt and pepper.
Put the kidneys and garlic into the oil when it is smoking hot
and cook very quickly, stirring all the time, for 3-4 minutes.
Do not overcook.
Squeeze the lemon juice over the kidneys and remove from
heat. Serve immediately on a bed of white rice.

Lemon Garlic Kidneys

Fried Brains in Lemon Sauce

4 pairs lamb brains
flour
2 beaten eggs
2 oz grated cheese
olive oil
salt

Soak the brains in water for 1 hour and drain. Bring some
salted water to the boil and pour it over the brains (in a
colander) and let them stand for 10 minutes.
Wipe the brains dry and cut into bite-sized pieces. Roll them
in flour, then egg, then finely grated cheese. Meanwhile, heat
plenty of oil in a deep frying pan or saucepan (it should be half
full), and fry the brains till they are golden brown. Drain on
absorbent paper, sprinkle with salt and serve immediately with the
following sauce.

Lemon Sauce

4 egg yolks
5 tablespoons lemon juice (strained)
3¾ tablespoons hot chicken broth (use a stock cube)

Beat the egg yolks till light and foaming then beat in the
lemon juice very slowly. When these ingredients are
completely blended, add the broth while still beating.
Cook this mixture over a low heat, stirring constantly,
until thick. The sauce must not boil or it will curdle.

Pork Chops with Cider

2 large, lean pork chops
2 shallots, finely chopped
1¼ tablespoons parsley, finely chopped
2 tablespoons melted butter
½ cup cider
salt
white pepper

Combine the shallots and parsley and season with salt and
pepper. Rub this mixture into both sides of the pork chops
which you have scored lightly.
Brush the chops with melted butter and broil the chops slowly
until tender.
Meanwhile, warm the cider in another pan and when the chops
have finished cooking put the broiling pan on top of the stove,
pour in the warmed cider and let it bubble over high heat for
a few minutes.
Serve hot with a simple green salad and mashed potatoes.

Chicken with Apricots

½ chicken
4 tablespoons oil
1 teaspoon flour
8 oz dried apricots, soaked overnight in water
2 cups liquid in which apricots were soaked
1¼ tablespoons minced onion
1 teaspoon sugar
salt
pepper

Cut the chicken into bite-sized pieces and sauté them in a
little oil in a saucepan until golden. Remove from the pan and
keep warm. Pour off all the oil except 1 tablespoon. Stir
the flour into the oil and gradually add 1 cup of the liquid
from the soaked apricots, stirring continuously. Add the
onion and cook for another 5 minutes.
Put the chicken pieces into this, add the sugar, salt and
pepper and half the apricots and enough of the apricot juice
to cover the chicken well. Cover and simmer gently until
the chicken is tender.
Just before serving, add the rest of the apricots and apricot
juice and reheat.
This dish improves if cooked the day before and reheated.

Chicken with Apricots

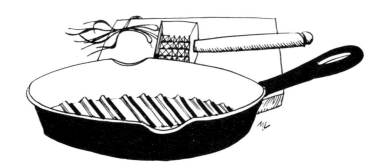

Curried Eggs

2 medium onions, sliced
1 small red chili
1 clove garlic, chopped and crushed
¾ cup chicken broth (use a stock cube)
½ teaspoon turmeric
1½ teaspoons curry powder
3 hard cooked eggs
good pinch salt

Combine onions, chili, garlic, broth, turmeric and curry
powder in a saucepan and simmer gently for 20-25 minutes.
Cut the eggs in half, add the eggs and a pinch of salt to the
curry mixture, and heat through gently.
Serve hot with plain boiled rice.

Spiced Chicken

half a chicken or several joints
1 teaspoon each ground cumin and coriander
¼ teaspoon ground cardamon
1 clove garlic, crushed
salt
½ cup plain yogurt

Trim chicken into neat joints.
Combine the spices, garlic and salt with the yogurt and
cover the chicken completely with this. For the best
results you should marinate the chicken for several hours.
Broil under a moderate heat on pieces of aluminium foil
to retain the juices for about half an hour, turning from
time to time.
Serve hot with saffron rice.

Stuffed Picnic Loaf

2 tomatoes, peeled and chopped
2 shallots or green onions, chopped
1 green pepper seeded, cored and chopped
a few black olives, with stones removed, then chopped
2 tablespoons capers
1 dill pickle, chopped
a small French loaf
pinch of sweet basil
olive oil
salt
freshly ground black pepper

This is ideal for a picnic and improves if made the day before.
Combine the tomatoes, shallots, green pepper, olives,
capers and dill pickle.
Cut the loaf in half lengthwise and scoop out all the bread.
Mix the bread with the tomato mixture along with a little
olive oil, basil, salt and pepper.
Fill the two empty bread shells with the mixture, press
together, wrap the loaf in aluminium foil, and chill.

Stuffed Picnic loaf

Chicken Stew

½ chicken
juice ½ lemon
pinch ground cloves
¼ teaspoon ground cinnamon
salt
pepper
6¼ tablespoons olive oil
3 tomatoes, peeled and chopped
1¼ tablespoons tomato paste
¾ cup hot water

Cut the chicken into about four pieces. Mix together the
lemon juice, cloves, cinnamon, salt and pepper and rub this
into the chicken.
Brown the chicken in the oil in a saucepan. Remove chicken
from the pan and keep hot. Put the tomato and tomato paste
in the pan, stir into the hot oil and add the hot water slowly.
Simmer over gentle heat until the tomato has softened.
Return the chicken to the saucepan, turning the pieces over
a few times to ensure they are covered with the sauce.
Cover and cook over medium heat till the meat is very
tender. Serve hot.

Paprika Chicken

1 onion, finely chopped
3 tablespoons butter
½ chicken
1 small tomato, peeled and finely chopped
salt
2 teaspoons paprika
2½ tablespoons flour
¼ cup sour cream

Gently fry onion in butter until soft.
Cut the chicken into bite-size pieces and add these to the
onion. Add the tomato.
Stir in a pinch of salt and the paprika and gradually add
enough water to cover. Simmer until the chicken is tender.
When the chicken is cooked, remove from the pan and keep
hot. Mix the flour into the sour cream and slowly add this
to the liquid, stirring continuously. Bring gently to the boil,
stirring all the time, return the chicken to the pan. Reheat.
Serve hot with noodles.

Sesame Chicken

2 chicken breasts, boned if possible
4 tablespoons melted butter
1¼ tablespoons soy sauce
½ teaspoon chopped tarragon
½ teaspoon mustard powder
1¼ tablespoons white wine
sesame seeds

Mix the butter, soy sauce, tarragon, mustard and wine.
Marinate the chicken in this for 3 hours. Drain and keep
the marinade.
Broil the chicken for 4-6 minutes each side. Remove from
heat, brush with the marinade, roll in sesame seeds and
return to heat until sesame seeds are brown.
Serve immediately.

Sesame Chicken

Chicken with Walnut Sauce

½ chicken, boiled
½ cup shelled walnuts
¼ cup shelled almonds
¼ cup shelled hazel nuts
paprika
salt
1 onion, chopped
3 tablespoons butter
½ cup chicken broth

Break the chicken into bite-sized pieces and keep hot.
Pound all the nuts together in a mortar with a pinch of
paprika and salt. Cook the chopped onion in the butter in a
saucepan, for 5 minutes. Add the nuts and chicken broth.
Simmer gently for 5 minutes.
Serve the chicken with the sauce over plain boiled rice.

Cold Chicken Veronique

½ chicken, boiled
1 egg yolk
¼ cup cream
2½ tablespoons sherry
finely shredded lemon peel
white grapes for garnish

A delicious way to use half a chicken.
Break the chicken into bite-sized pieces, discarding the
bones.
Beat the egg yolk with the cream and sherry. Cook,
stirring all the time, over a gentle heat until the sauce has
thickened slightly. Pour this over the chicken and sprinkle
with lemon peel.
Decorate with white grapes. Serve chilled.

Stuffed Fillet of Beef

1 lb fillet of beef
2 onions, sliced
beef dripping
2 anchovy fillets, chopped
1¼ tablespoons finely chopped bacon
pepper
pinch thyme
pinch finely chopped parsley
1 egg yolk, beaten

Trim the beef neatly.
Slice the onions and sauté them in about 1¼ tablespoons of
dripping, until they are golden. Remove them from the pan,
place in a mixing bowl and add the anchovy fillets, bacon,
pinch pepper, thyme and parsley and the beaten egg yolk.
Slice the fillet in about 4 places, but not all the way through.
Put some of the stuffing into each cavity and tie the fillet.
Either wrap in foil and place in a roasting pan or place in
a covered pan with a little dripping and cook in a slow oven
(250°F) for 1½ hours or until tender.
Serve hot, cut into thick slices, accompanied by freshly cooked
vegetables.

Mayonnaise

1 egg yolk
salt
olive oil, about ½ cup
lemon juice

Whisk the yolk well using a wooden spoon with a pinch of
salt, then, as you continue stirring in the same direction all
the time, add the oil slowly drop by drop until the mayonnaise
is like a very thick custard. Add strained lemon juice drop by
drop, until the mayonnaise is to your taste.
Should the mixture curdle, put another beaten egg yolk into
a clean bowl and, using a clean spoon, gradually stir in
curdled mayonnaise.

A tasty variation on the ordinary mayonnaise is aioli, a
garlic mayonnaise which is very pleasant (*if* you're keen on
garlic) with plain, hot, boiled vegetables such as green beans,
small new potatoes, carrots and zucchini.
To make aioli: Prepare mayonnaise in usual way, but add
about 4 finely chopped and pounded garlic cloves to the egg
yolk before adding the oil. Add plenty of chopped parsley to
the finished mayonnaise.

Egg Mayonnaise

3 hard-cooked eggs
mayonnaise
chopped parsley

Pour a generous amount of good, home-made mayonnaise
into a shallow bowl and place on it the shelled, hard-cooked
eggs cut in half lengthwise and placed cut side down. Sprinkle
with a little finely chopped parsley.
Serve slightly chilled with salad.

Ratatouille with Eggs

2 medium potatoes
3 small zucchini
2 medium tomatoes
2 medium onions, peeled
2 cloves garlic, sliced
1 green pepper, seeded
¼ cup olive oil
salt and pepper
2 eggs

Wash all the vegetables. Peel the potatoes and the tomatoes.
Cut the ends off the zucchini.
Slice all the vegetables.
Heat the olive oil in a heavy pan, add the vegetables, season
to taste and simmer, covered, for 30 minutes. Simmer for a
further 20 minutes with the pan uncovered.
Serve on individual dishes topped with a fried egg.

Rumanian Omelet with Herbs

3 eggs
salt and pepper
5 tablespoons yogurt or sour cream
2½ level tablespoons flour
1¼ tablespoons finely chopped sorrel, tarragon, parsley or chives
2 tablespoons butter

Beat the eggs lightly, season to taste and whisk in the yogurt
or sour cream.
Sift the flour into a bowl and lightly stir in the egg and yogurt
mixture and the herbs.
Heat half the butter in a heavy frying pan and pour in half the
mixture. Cook over a low heat, moving the eggs around to
prevent them burning. When brown underneath turn and cook
the other side.
Slide cooked omelet onto a warmed plate and serve at once topped
with a nut of butter.
Cook another in the same manner.

Rumanian Omelet with herbs.

Salads & Vegetables

Garbanzo (Chick Pea) Salad

1 cup garbanzos (chick peas)
2 tablespoons cooking salt.
1 tablespoon flour
freshly ground black pepper
salt
olive oil
a little finely sliced onion

Soak the garbanzos overnight in tepid water in which you
have put a few tablespoons of cooking salt and a tablespoon
of flour.
Next day remove the garbanzos from the water in which they
have soaked, but keep the water. Bring the water to a boil,
add a pinch of bicarbonate·of soda, then set aside to cool.
When it is cold, add the rinsed peas, bring to the boil then
simmer gently for an hour. Strain, discard the original water
and put the peas into a large saucepan with plenty of fresh,
lightly salted, boiling water, and cook until quite tender.
While the peas are still warm, season to taste, add olive oil
and a little finely sliced onion.
Serve cold.

Coleslaw

2 cups thinly sliced cabbage (about ¼ cabbage)
2½ tablespoons oil
1¼ tablespoons vinegar
½ teaspoon sugar
½ apple, chopped but not peeled
1¼ tablespoons raisins

Combine all ingredients well and chill, covered, for several hours before serving.
Turn the coleslaw occasionally while it is in the refrigerator.

Armenian Cucumbers

1 cucumber, peeled and roughly chopped
1 level teaspoon salt
1¼ tablespoons white wine vinegar
1 clove garlic, finely chopped and crushed
8 oz plain yogurt
1½ teaspoons cumin seed
1 teaspoon chopped mint

A delicious and refreshingly different salad idea, ideal with a curry.
Prepare the cucumber and put into serving dish. Combine the salt, vinegar and garlic and stir into the yogurt. Stir in the cumin seed and mint and pour over the cucumber. Chill before serving.

Salade Niçoise

½ head of lettuce, cut into 4 wedges
1 hard-cooked egg, halved
1 very firm medium sized tomato cut into quarters
a few anchovy fillets
4 black olives
4 capers
¼ green pepper sliced
a little chopped basil
olive oil
1¼ tablespoons tarragon vinegar
salt and freshly ground black pepper
1 clove garlic, crushed and minced

Arrange all the ingredients except the basil, oil, vinegar, salt
and pepper and garlic on a plate (not in a dish or salad bowl)
Just before serving pour over a dressing made by shaking
together the remaining ingredients (except for the basil).
Sprinkle the basil lightly over the salad.

Salade Niçoise

Tomato and Rice Salad

½ cup raw white rice
salt
1 slice lemon
2½ tablespoons olive oil
2 teaspoons tarragon vinegar
salt
nutmeg
2 large ripe tomatoes, skinned and sliced
chopped parsley

Cook the rice in plenty of boiling salted water to which a
slice of lemon has been added, until tender. Drain the rice,
discard the lemon and immediately stir in the olive oil,
vinegar, a pinch of salt and a pinch of nutmeg.
Arrange the tomato on top of the rice and garnish with
parsley. Chill before serving.

Spinach Salad

½ lb spinach
a few cold, boiled potatoes, thinly sliced
3 slices Gruyère cheese, cut into strips
1¼ tablespoons cream
juice ¼ lemon
salt
freshly ground black pepper

Cook the spinach, from which you have removed the hard
white stems, in boiling water for 3 minutes.
Drain and mix with the cold potatoes, cheese, cream, lemon
juice and salt and pepper to taste.
Serve hot or cold.

Green Bean Salad

½ lb green beans (preferably the thin, stringless variety)
1 clove garlic, finely chopped and crushed
2½ tablespoons olive oil
2 teaspoons lemon juice
salt and freshly ground black pepper

Wash and chop the beans into 2-inch pieces. Cook in boiling, salted water till tender.
Drain the beans and place in a bowl which has been rubbed with garlic. Stir in the oil and add the lemon juice. Season with black pepper, taste and add salt if necessary. Chill before serving.

Peperoni

2 green peppers
3¾ tablespoons olive oil
1¼ tablespoons lemon juice or white wine vinegar
salt
1 clove of garlic, chopped and crushed
parsley

Skin the peppers by holding them over a gas flame or placing
them under the broiler, turning them constantly until the
skin is charred black. The skin will rub off easily under cold
running water. Remove every last piece of skin and also the
seeds and cores. Cut the peppers into long strips, add a little
olive oil and vinegar, season with salt and add the garlic and
a little chopped parsley.
Chill well.

Preparation of julienne strips for **Peperoni**

Small Potato Pancakes

4 medium cold boiled potatoes (peeled)
1 tablespoon melted butter
salt
freshly ground black pepper
1 teaspoon finely chopped parsley
1 shallot or green onion, finely chopped
4 tablespoons grated Parmesan cheese
½ cup flour
2 tomatoes, peeled and finely chopped
oil

Mash the potatoes and put through a coarse sieve. Mix in the
melted butter, salt, pepper, parsley, shallot and cheese and
tomatoes (press out any excess liquid first) and the flour.
Knead gently, roll out to ½ inch thick and cut out rounds
3 to 4-inches in diameter.
Heat some oil and fry the potato cakes till they are golden
brown on each side. Drain well and serve.

Vegetable Casserole

2 green peppers
½ lb green beans
2 onions, peeled and chopped
1 clove garlic, chopped and crushed
½ cup olive oil
1 ripe tomato, peeled and chopped
¬2 medium potatoes, peeled and chopped
freshly ground black pepper
sour cream or yogurt for topping

Remove the tops from the green peppers, discard white
cores and seeds. Cut into rounds about ¼-inch wide. Cut
the beans in half.
Sauté the onions and garlic in the oil in a heavy saucepan
until they become transparent. Add tomato, beans, green
pepper and potatoes. Add pepper to taste. Put a very tight lid
on the pan, bring quickly to the boil and then reduce the
heat and simmer slowly until the vegetables are quite soft.
Serve hot topped with sour cream or yogurt.

Sweet and Sour Cabbage

½ a small red cabbage
1 green cooking apple, peeled, cored and sliced thinly
1 onion, sliced thinly
salt
freshly ground black pepper
1¼ tablespoons sugar
sprig of parsley
bay leaf
pinch of thyme
1¼ tablespoons port
1¼ tablespoons wine vinegar

A very nice accompaniment to pork.
Take the tough outside leaves off the cabbage, cut out the
stalk and cut the cabbage into two quarters. Slice thinly.
Put the cabbage in a casserole, making alternate layers of
cabbage, onion and apple. Season each layer with salt and
pepper and sugar as you go. Put the herbs in the middle
layer. When you have used all the cabbage, onion and
apple, pour in the wine and vinegar. Cook, covered, in a
low oven for about 2 hours. Serve hot.

Sweet and Sour Cabbage

Orange Mint Salad

2 sweet, thin-skinned navel oranges
1¼ tablespoons finely chopped mint
3¾ tablespoons olive oil
2 teaspoons lemon juice
2 teaspoons Cognac

Peel and pith the oranges.
Slice oranges, discard ends and arrange slices overlappling on
a plate. Sprinkle with mint. Combine oil, lemon juice and
Cognac and pour over the oranges. Chill before serving.

Carrots Vichy

1 lb small new carrots
2 tablespoons butter
pinch salt
2 teaspoons sugar
1 cup water
pinch bicarbonate of soda
a little finely chopped parsley

Scrape the carrots and cut into ¼-inch thick rounds.
Cook in a small heavy pan with half the butter, salt, sugar,
water and bicarbonate of soda.
Cook with the saucepan uncovered until the carrots are
tender and almost all of the water has evaporated. If there
is any water left in the pan, drain it off. Add the rest of the
butter and shake the pan to prevent the carrots sticking.
Serve immediately garnished with a little finely chopped
parsley.

Orange Mint Salad and Carrots Vichy

Mushrooms in Cream Sauce

½ lb mushrooms
2 tablespoons butter
1¼ tablespoons olive oil
salt
freshly ground black pepper
pinch nutmeg
1¼ tablespoons finely chopped parsley
½ shallot or green onion, finely chopped
4 tablespoons heavy cream

Wipe mushrooms clean and slice thinly.
Heat butter and oil in a frying pan (skillet) and cook
mushrooms over medium heat for a minute then add salt,
pepper, nutmeg, parsley and shallot. Move the mushrooms
around a little to prevent their sticking to the pan.
Stir in the cream and continue cooking gently for 5
minutes. Serve immediately.

Potatoes Dauphinois

4 medium potatoes
1 cup cream
1 clove garlic, crushed
butter

Peel the potatoes and slice into thin rounds. Wash them in
cold water and dry lightly in a towel.
Arrange potato slices in layers in a shallow ovenproof dish
rubbed with the garlic and well buttered. Season to taste.
Pour the cream over them and dot with butter. Bake for about
1½ hours in a slow oven (250-300°F).
To obtain a crust on the potatoes, turn the oven up to high
for the last 10 minutes.

Desserts

Melon and Grapes

1 honeydew melon or cantaloupe
sugar
lemon juice
1 small bunch seedless grapes

Cut melon into wedges, peel off the rind and discard the
seeds. Cut melon into cubes and put cubes in a serving bowl.
Sprinkle with sugar and lemon juice to taste.
Wash and slightly crush the grapes and add to the melon.
Serve cold.

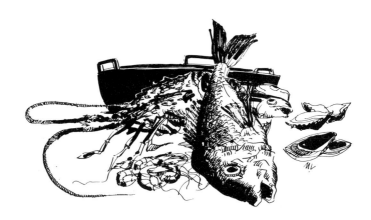

Melon & Grapes

Pears in Cream

3 firm pears
1 tablespoon butter
3 tablespoons vanilla sugar
4 tablespoons heavy cream

Peel, core, slice and quarter the pears.
Melt the butter in a shallow ovenproof dish, big enough to
take all the pears in one layer. Add the pears and the sugar
and cook very gently over low heat until the pears are
tender (anything from 10-25 minutes, depending on how
ripe the pears are).
Add the cream and cook for 2 minutes, shaking the pan until
the cream becomes thick.
Place in a moderate oven for 5 minutes. Serve hot.
Note: For Vanilla sugar, see page 114.

Pears in Red Wine

2 fresh, very firm pears
red wine
1 whole clove
1 small stick of cinnamon, crushed
3 tablespoons sugar
1 tablespoon brandy or Cognac

Carefully peel the pears, leaving on the stalks. Place the pears
in a deep saucepan, just wide enough to accommodate them.
Pour in enough wine to cover, add the clove, cinnamon and
sugar and cook over a low heat until tender. Carefully remove
the pears and serve with some of the liquid plus ½ tablespoon
of brandy or Cognac poured over each serving.
Serve hot or cold.

Apples with Calvados

3 Granny Smith apples, peeled, cored and thinly sliced
3 tablespoons butter
2½ tablespoons vanilla sugar
¼ cup Calvados

Gently cook the apples in the melted butter with the
sugar in a frying pan (skillet) until pale golden and almost
transparent. When turning the slices do so gently so as
not to break them.
When tender, flame with the Calvados (warm it over a flame
in a soup ladle or spoon, ignite and pour over the apples).
When the flames go out, serve immediately.

Note: Vanilla sugar is castor sugar which is flavoured with a
vanilla bean. You may make it yourself by placing a vanilla
bean in a jar of castor sugar or you may buy it from leading
food stores.

Strawberry Whip

1 pint box strawberries
¾ cup thick cream
1 egg white, stiffly beaten
1¼ tablespoons fruit sugar (more or less depending on how
sweet the fruit is)

Hull the strawberries, put aside six and mash the rest to a
pulp.
Whip the cream, fold in the stiffly beaten egg white, then
the mashed strawberries. Stir in the sugar.
Pile the cream in individual goblets and decorate with the
whole strawberries.

Pineapple with Kirsch

half a small ripe pineapple
superfine sugar
1¼ tablespoons Kirsch

Core and peel the pineapple and cut into ½-inch slices and
then bite-sized wedges.
Arrange on a flat round dish, sprinkle with castor sugar and
kirsch, and serve.

Fried Bananas with Rum

2 large bananas
2 tablespoons butter
juice of ¼ of a lemon
2 tablespoons rum (or brandy)
fruit sugar

Melt the butter in a frying pan (skillet) and as it begins to
bubble, put in the bananas which have been peeled and cut in
half lengthwise. Cook them very gently on both sides for 2
minutes, add the lemon juice. Flame with the rum or brandy (warm
it in a ladle or spoon, ignite and pour over the bananas).
Sprinkle with sugar and serve immediately; delicious with
cream.

Bananas with Kirsch and Cream

2 large ripe bananas
sugar
2 teaspoons Kirsch
2½ tablespoons thick cream

Slice the bananas, sprinkle with sugar and Kirsch and stir in the
cream. Mix gently, but thoroughly, to ensure that the
bananas are properly coated with the mixture. Serve at room
temperature.

Peaches in Wine

2 large, ripe, unblemished, freestone peaches
fruit sugar
lemon juice
red wine or white dessert wine

Peel peaches carefully and slice into goblets.
Sprinkle the peaches with plenty of sugar and a little lemon
juice. Just before serving, pour enough wine into the goblets
to just reach the top of the fruit.

Peaches in Wine

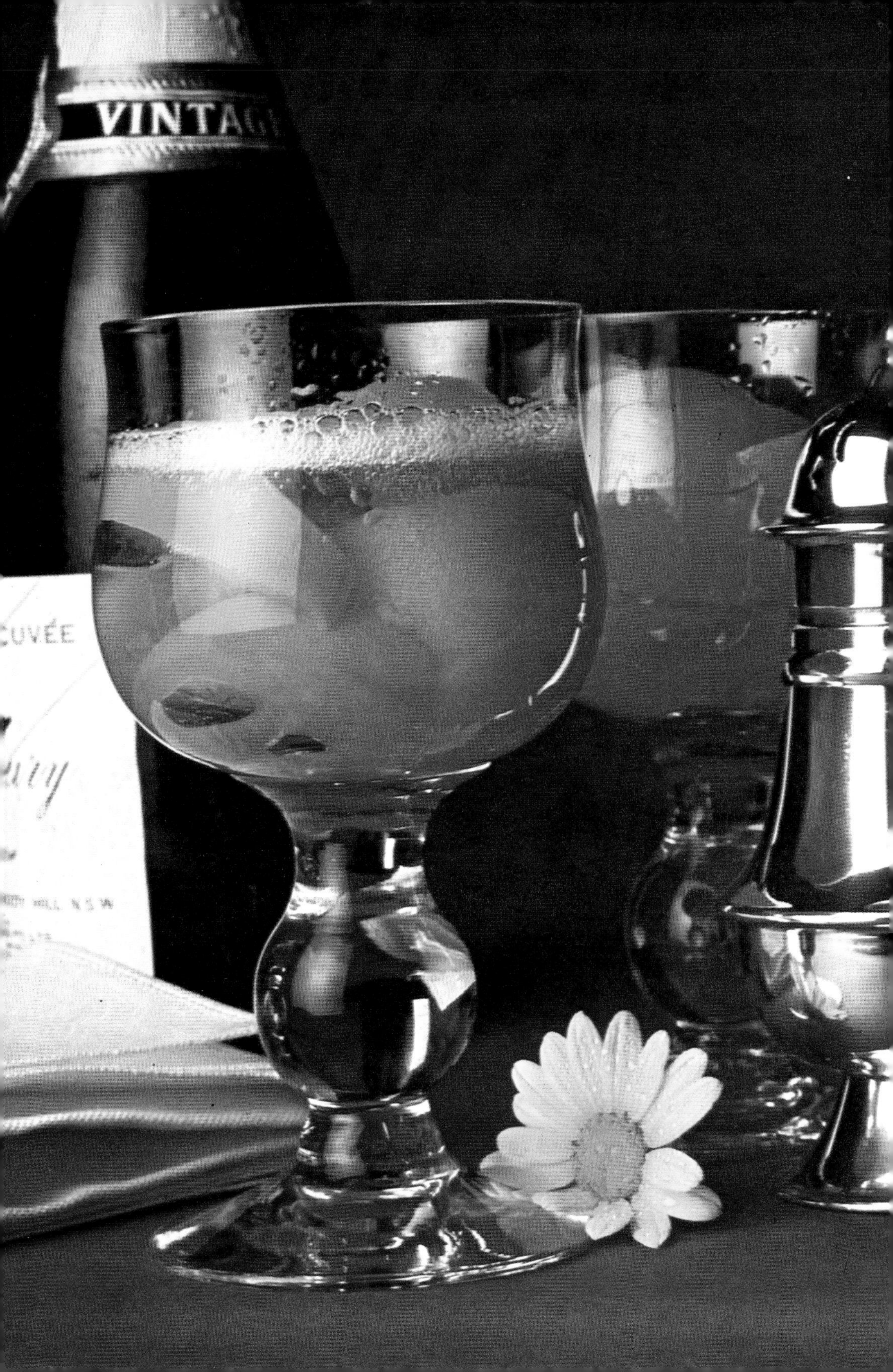
VINTAG
CUVÉE

Rich Egg Custard

1 cup milk
2 eggs
2 tablespoons sugar
nutmeg

Beat the eggs, sugar and milk well. Pour into a small buttered ovenproof dish and sprinkle lightly with nutmeg.
Place in a baking dish filled with enough cold water to come half way up the side of the ovenproof dish and bake uncovered in a slow oven (275-300°F.) until custard is set, about 45 minutes. Serve hot or cold with canned or stewed fruit. If serving hot, cool slightly for 10 minutes.

Orange Whip

2 cups orange juice
1 envelope plain gelatin
2½ tablespoons sugar
2 eggs, separated

Soak the gelatin in the orange juice for 30 minutes. Heat the orange juice and gelatin, stirring constantly, just until it starts to boil, then remove from heat and pour through a sieve over the well beaten egg yolks. Stir well then cool.
When the mixture has started to thicken, beat the egg whites until they peak then fold them into the soufflé.
Chill well and serve with cream.

Chocolate-Orange Mousse

2 oz bitter chocolate (2 squares)
2 eggs, separated
1 tablespoon soft butter
juice of ½ an orange
½ teaspoon Grand Marnier

Break the chocolate into pieces and soften by placing in an
ovenproof dish in a slow oven or in a pan over gently
boiling water.
When the chocolate is quite soft, stir in the well-beaten
yolks of the eggs, the soft butter and the orange juice and
Grand Marnier — in that order
Beat the egg whites till they form peaks and fold into the
chocolate mixture. Pour into individual serving dishes and
chill before serving.

Berry Mold

1 cup strawberries
1 cup fresh black cherries
1 Granny Smith apple
½ cup sugar
sliced white bread or sliced raisin loaf
cream for serving

Put the fruit in a pan with the sugar (use more or less
depending on how sweet the fruit is. Heat very gently
until the juice flows from the fruit, moving the fruit
constantly to prevent it sticking. Crush the fruit slightly.
Butter the inside of a small pudding bowl and line with thin
slices of crustless bread. Fill with the fruit and top with
more bread.
Butter the bottom of a small plate that will fit into the top
of the bowl and place the plate on top of the pudding and
put a weight on top of this. Chill overnight. Turn out and
serve with cream.

Berry Mold

Chocolate Semolina

1¼ cups milk
1¼ tablespoons cocoa
2½ tablespoons sugar
2½ tablespoons semolina
3 drops vanilla essence
2 tablespoons butter
1 egg

Mix a little of the measured milk in a small bowl with the cocoa and sugar, to form a smooth paste.
Bring remainder of milk to boil in a saucepan. Sprinkle in semolina and cocoa mixture and bring to the boil stirring continuously.
Simmer over a low heat for 1-2 minutes.
Remove from heat and stir in vanilla, butter and beaten egg.
Pour into a small, greased pie dish and bake in a moderate oven (350-375° F.) for 20-25 minutes.
Serve hot with pouring cream if desired.

Superman Special

1¼ cups milk
1¼ tablespoons castor sugar
2 tablespoons butter
1 cup cake crumbs
1 egg
3 drops vanilla essence
2½ tablespoons sultanas

Place milk in a saucepan with sugar and butter and bring just to the boil.
Cook for 5 minutes than stir in cake crumbs.

124

Beat egg, add vanilla and stir into basic mixture along with sultanas.
Pour into two individual greased ovenproof dishes or a small pie dish and place in a baking dish. Pour in water to cover half way up pudding dishes.
Bake in a moderate oven (350-375°F.) for 40-45 minutes.
Serve hot or cold.

Country Junket

2½ cups fresh milk
2 junket tablets or 1 tablespoon essence of rennet
1¼ tablespoons superfine sugar
1¼ tablespoons rum
¼ teaspoon ground nutmeg
¼ teaspoon ground cinnamon
strawberry jam and whipped cream for serving

Make junket with lukewarm milk and junket tablets, according to directions on bottle.
Stir in sugar, rum and spices and pour into a warm bowl.
Leave to set at room temperature, ½ − 1 hour.
Serve topped with strawberry jam and whipped cream.

Cream Trifle

¾ cups heavy cream
1¼ tablespoons golden syrup
2½ tablespoons rum
2 sponge fingers
sliced strawberries or Chinese gooseberries for decoration
juice of 1 small lemon

Pour cream into a small mixing bowl and mix in warmed golden syrup and rum.
Slice sponge fingers or lamingtons and place in the bottom of two individual serving bowls.
Pour cream mixture over and cover with sliced fruit.
Chill for 1 hour.
Sprinkle lemon juice over just before serving.

Index